Anno's Magical A B C
an anamorphic alphabet
Mitsumasa Anno & Masaichiro Anno

PHILOMEL BOOKS   *NEW YORK*

Library of Congress Cataloging in Publication Data

Anno, Mitsumasa, 1926
Anno's magical abc.
  SUMMARY: The distorted letters of the alphabet
become quite clear when viewed with the help of the
silver tube included with the book.
    1. English language – Alphabet – Juvenile literature.
2. Anamorphic art – Juvenile literature. [1. Alphabet.
2. Toy and movable books] I. Anno, Masaichiro,
joint author. II. Title.
PE1155.A5 1981   421'.1   80–26024
ISBN 0–399–20788–0

What is anamorphosis?

When you stand in front of a funny mirror in an amusement park the reflection of your face and body is distorted. In a concave mirror you look short and fat, in a cylindrical mirror you look tall and thin. The same is true, of course, of a reflected drawing or painting, and with a drawing or painting you can reverse the process. If you draw something warped and misshapen in a particular way and then look at it in a distorted mirror, its reflected image will look quite normal. This method of drawing is called anamorphosis and its purpose is solely to mystify and amuse.

The word anamorphosis seems first to have been used in the 17th century but the underlying principle of negative perspective was understood long before that by ancient Greek painters and sculptors who distorted the proportions of works designed to be exhibited in raised positions so that they would look normal when viewed from below. Anamorphosis was once very popular in Europe and two fine examples of anamorphosis in painting are the portrait of Edward VI in the National Portrait Gallery in London, attributed to Cornelis Anthonisz in 1546, and the distorted skull in Holbein's Ambassadors (1533) in the National Gallery in London. In Japan, too, during the Edo Period of 1600–1868 there was a type of anamorphic picture which was drawn to be reflected on the sheath of a sword. In the middle of this book you will find an explanation of how you can do your own anamorphic painting or drawing.

How to look at this book

Every new copy of *Anno's Magical ABC* has two sheets of mirror paper in a pocket inside the cover. Tape the paper around a drinking glass, an empty can, a bottle or a similar cylindrical object, and stand it in the middle of the page. Both the letter and the picture will spring into focus in the mirror. Keep the mirror paper clean by wiping it with a soft cloth.

If the original sheets of mirror paper have been used or lost, here are a number of alternative suggestions:

* Take the label off a can of soup (or baked beans or anything) and use the can as a reflector.
* Stand a new roll of aluminum foil in the middle of the page. It must be new because once the foil is unrolled it creases and spoils the reflection.
* Buy new sheets of mirror paper at an art supply shop, or stainless steel or aluminum sheets at a hardware shop.

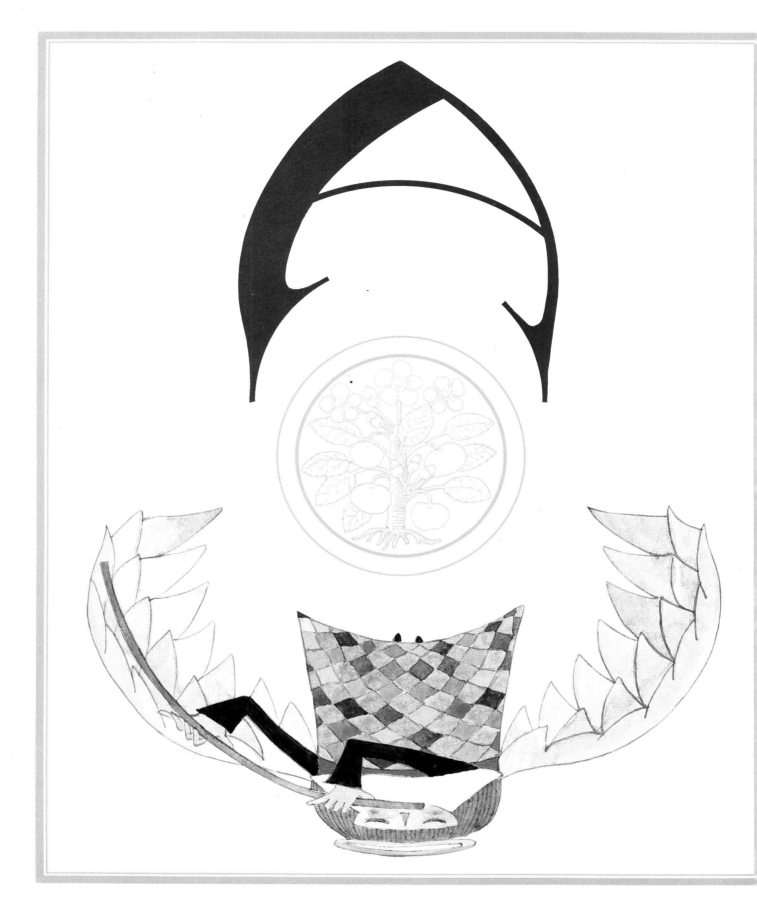

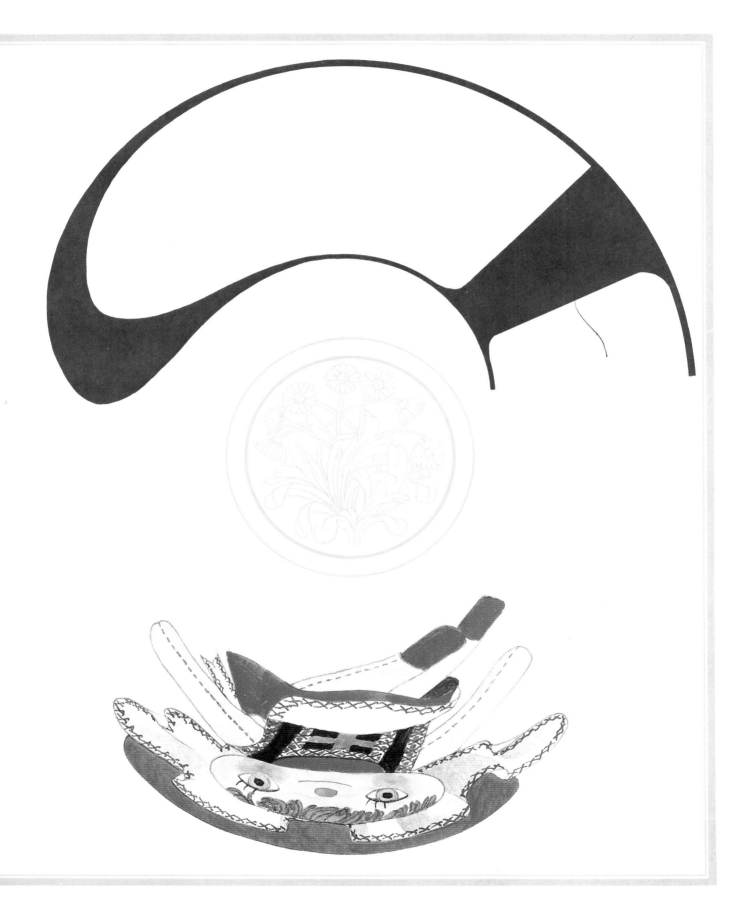

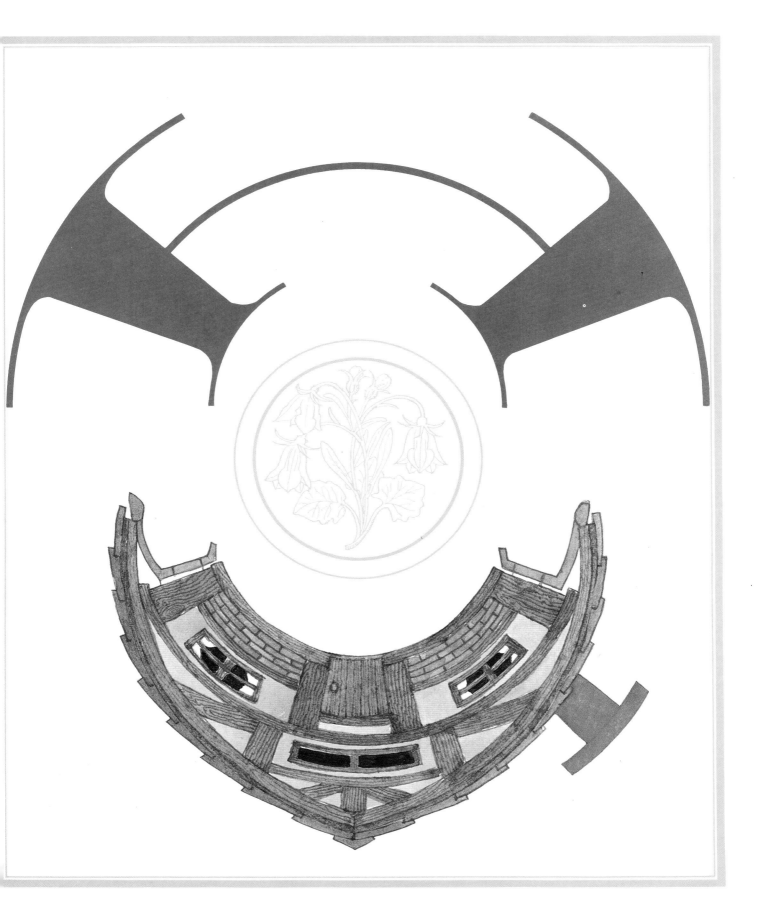

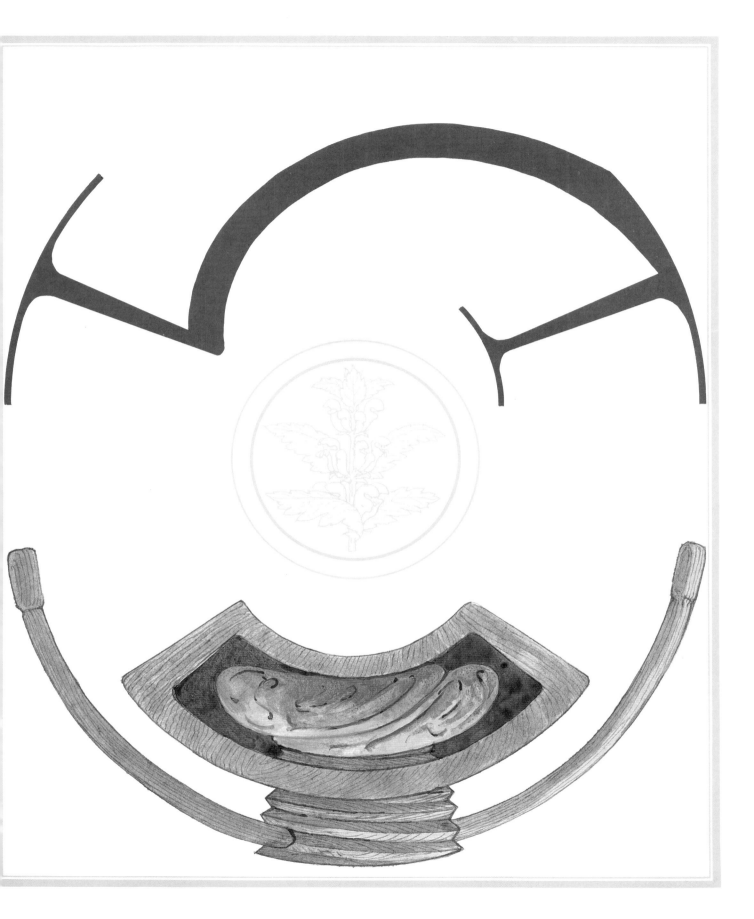

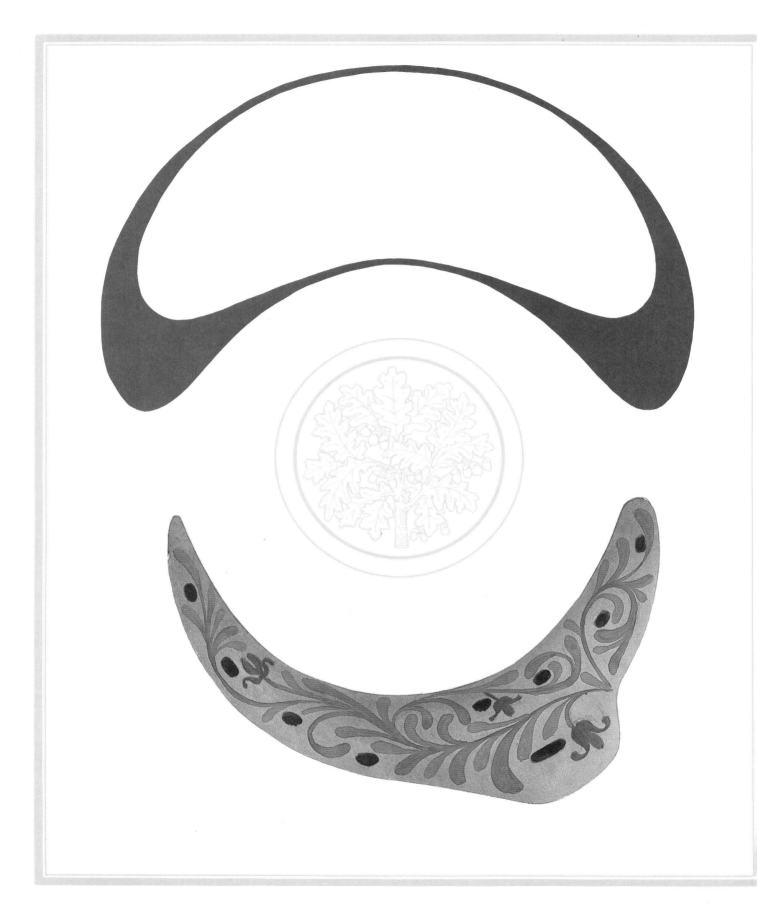

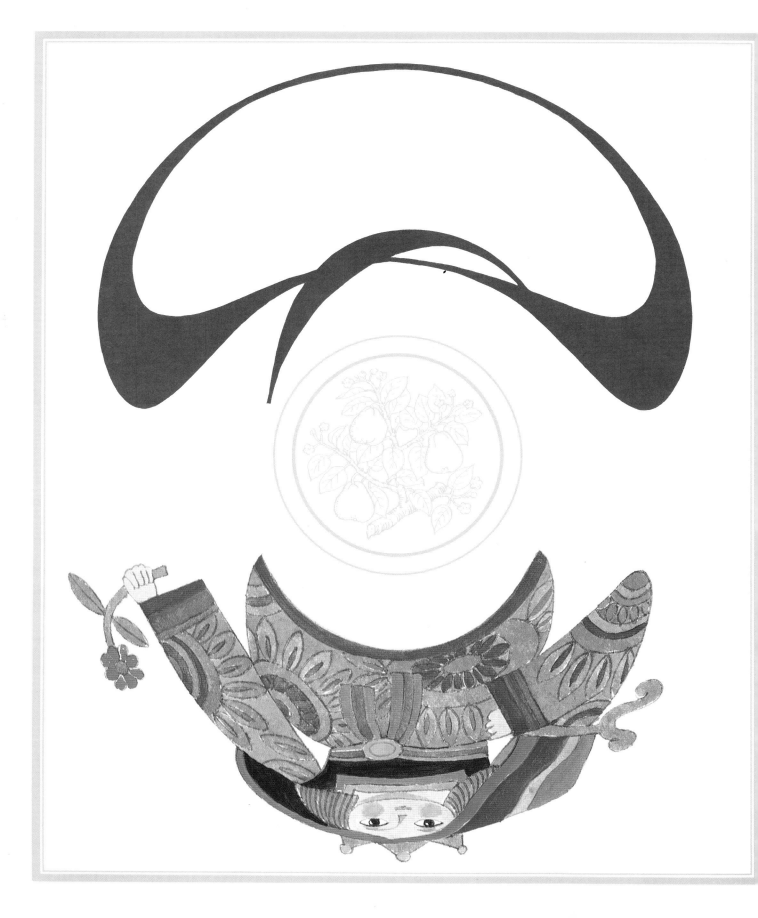

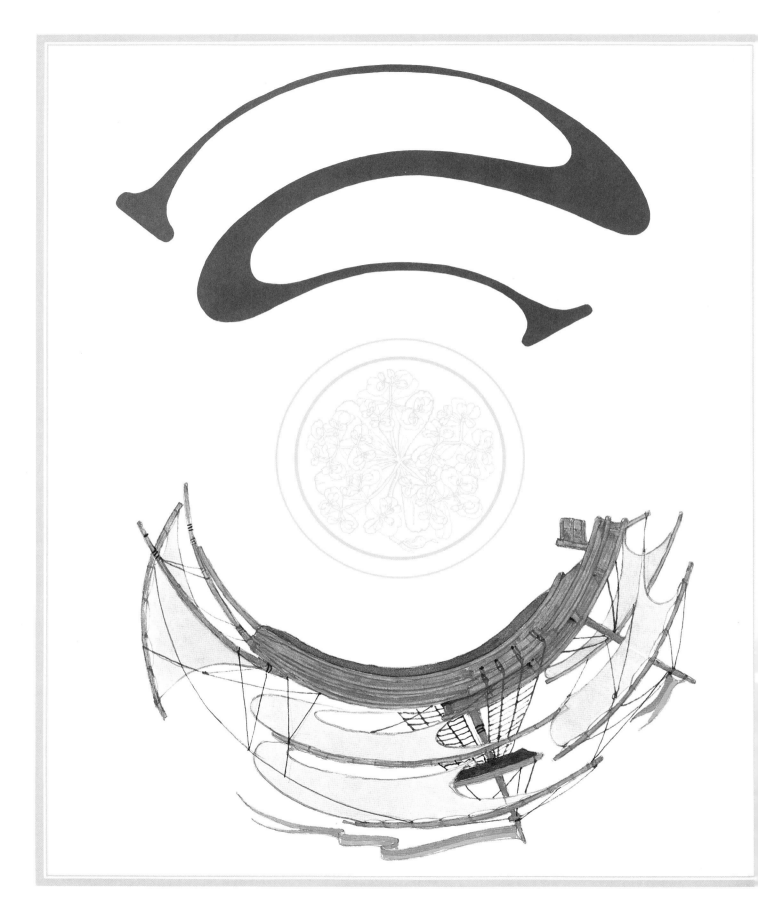

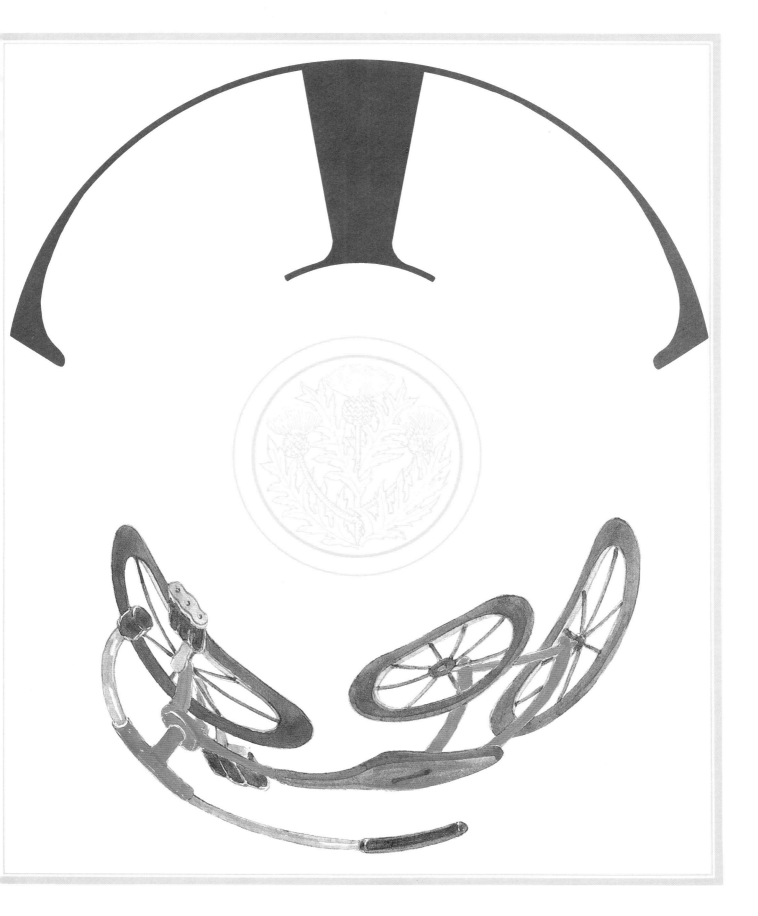

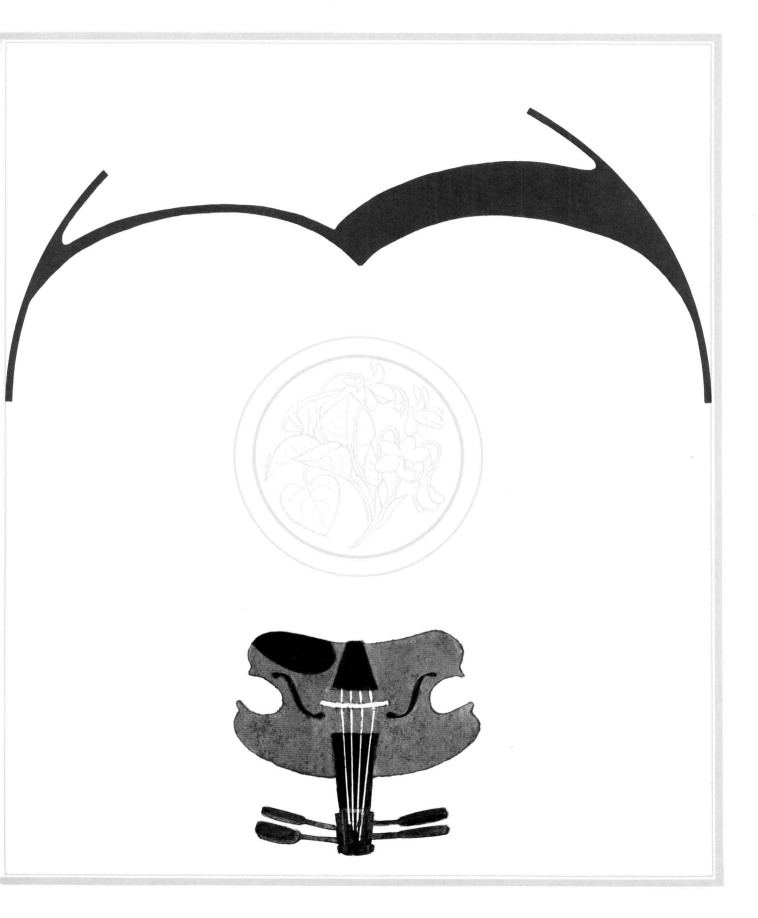

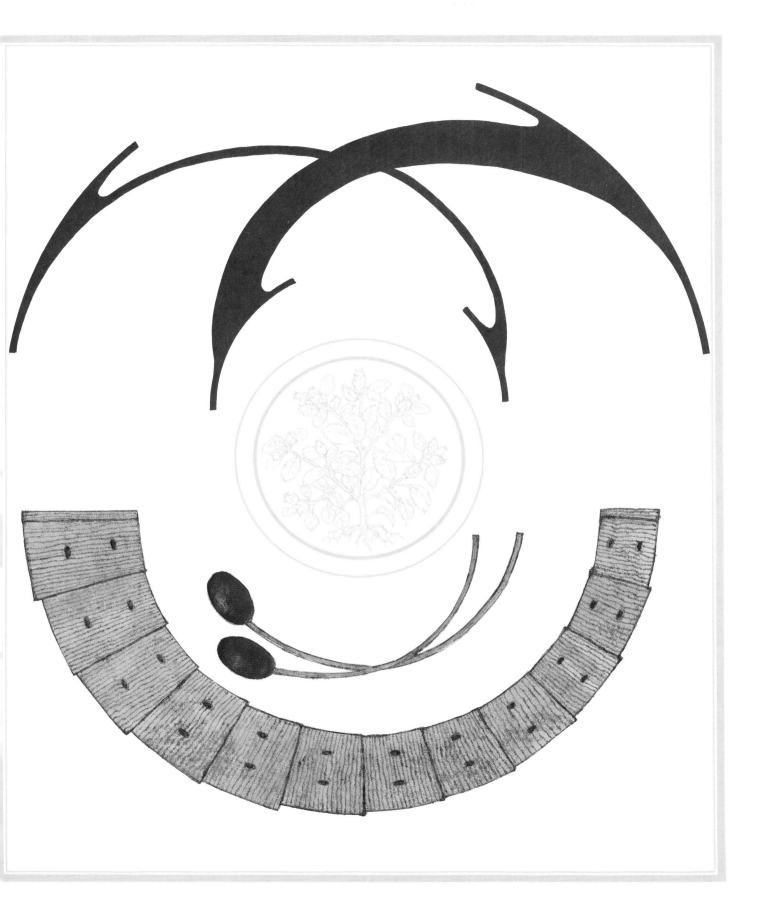

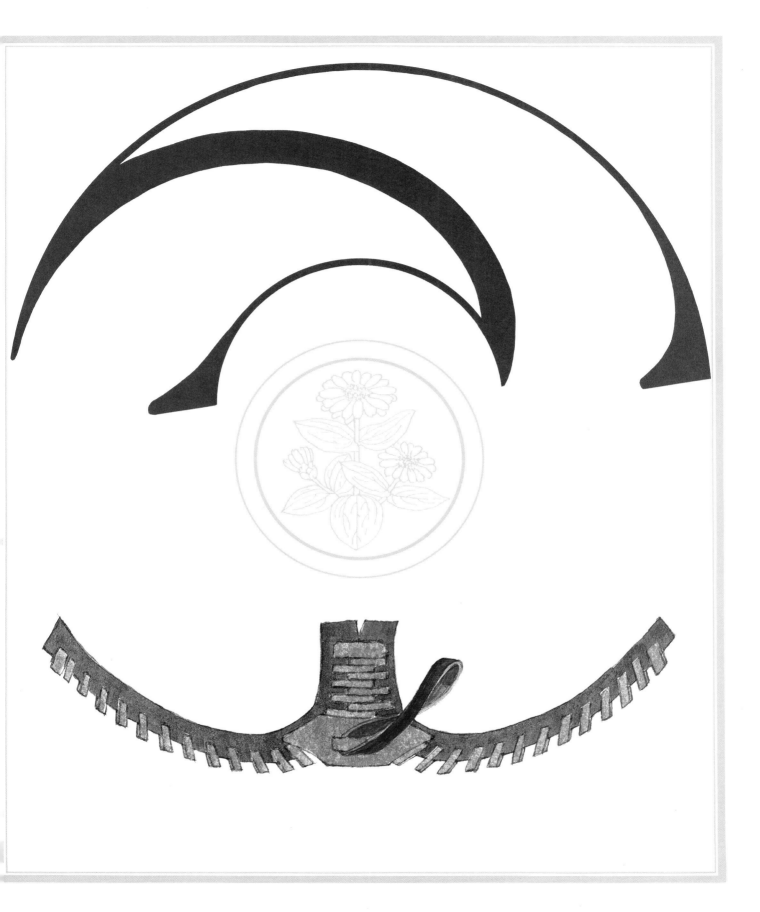

Clues to Anno's spells

A	Angel 天使	ant, anteater アリ、アリクイ	apple リンゴ
B	Balalaika バラライカ	bee, bear ハチ、クマ	blackberry クロイチゴ
C	Cassette カセットテープ	camel ラクダ	clover クローバー
D	Doll 人形	donkey ロバ	daisy デージー、ヒナギク
E	Elf, Egg 小びと、たまご	elephant ゾウ	elm ニレ
F	Faun フォーン牧神 (ローマ神話の半人半羊の林野牧畜の神) ギリシャ神話ではPan	fox キツネ	forget-me-not ワスレナグサ
G	Glider グライダー	goat ヤギ	gentian リンドウ
H	House 家	horse ウマ	harebell (= bluebell) イトシャジン
I	Ice cream アイスクリーム	iguana イグアナ	ivy ツタ
J	Jack ジャック	jaguar ジャガー	jasmine ジャスミン
K	King キング	kangaroo カンガルー	knobble knapweed ヤグルマギクのなかま
L	Lamp ランプ	lion ライオン	lily ユリ
M	Mermaid 人魚	mouse ネズミ	millet キビ
N	Nut-cracker くるみ割り	newt イモリ	nettle イラクサ
O	Ocarina オカリナ	ox ウシ	oak カシの木
P	Pirate 海賊	pig ブタ	poppy ポピー、ケシ
Q	Queen クィーン	quail ウズラ	quince マルメロ
R	Racquet ラケット	rabbit ウサギ	rose バラ
S	Ship 帆船	squirrel リス	sun spurge トウダイグサ
T	Tricycle 三輪車	tiger トラ	thistle アザミ
U	Umbrella かさ	unicorn ユニコーン、一角獣	*urtica pilulifera* (= roman nettle) イラクサのなかま
V	Violin バイオリン	vulture ハゲタカ	violet スミレ
W	Windmill 風車	wolf オオカミ	walnut クルミの木
X	Xylophone 木琴	*xenus cinerius* (= terek sandpiper) ソリハシシギ	*xanthium strumarium* (= lesser burdock) オナモミ
Y	Yacht ヨット	yak ヤク	yew イチイ
Z	Zipper ジッパー	zebra シマウマ	zinnia ヒャクニチソウ

About Mitsumasa Anno

Mitsumasa Anno was born in 1926 in Tsuwano, a small historic town in the western part of Japan. He graduated from Yamaguchi Teacher Training College and then worked as a primary school teacher before starting his career as an artist. Mr. Anno now lives in Tokyo but he is a regular traveler to Europe and has visited the United States of America. A selection of his illustrations from 1968–1977 has been published as *The Unique World of Mitsumasa Anno* – and his many picture books for children include:

Anno's Animals
Anno's Journey
Anno's Italy
Anno's Medieval World
The King's Flower

How to do an anamorphic drawing

Anamorphosis is not easy, but it is great fun. The reduced graphs on this page show you how it is done. On Graph A, the letter K has been drawn in reverse and then transferred to Graph B, box by box. By now it is hard to figure out what it is, but when reflected in a cylindrical mirror it will come back to its normal shape again.

You can draw an anamorphic picture in exactly the same way. First, trace out copies of the enlarged graphs from the opposite page, or make photocopies of them, so you can experiment as often as you like and still leave the printed graphs clean for the next person. Now draw your picture straightforwardly on your copy of Graph A and then transfer it, box by box, to your copy of Graph B. It is important to remember that letters and pictures have to be drawn in reverse because the reflected images will be seen from the other way up. Good luck.

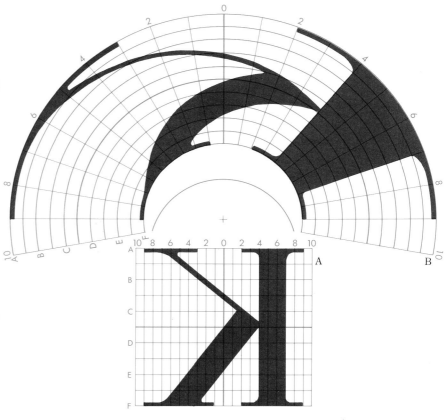

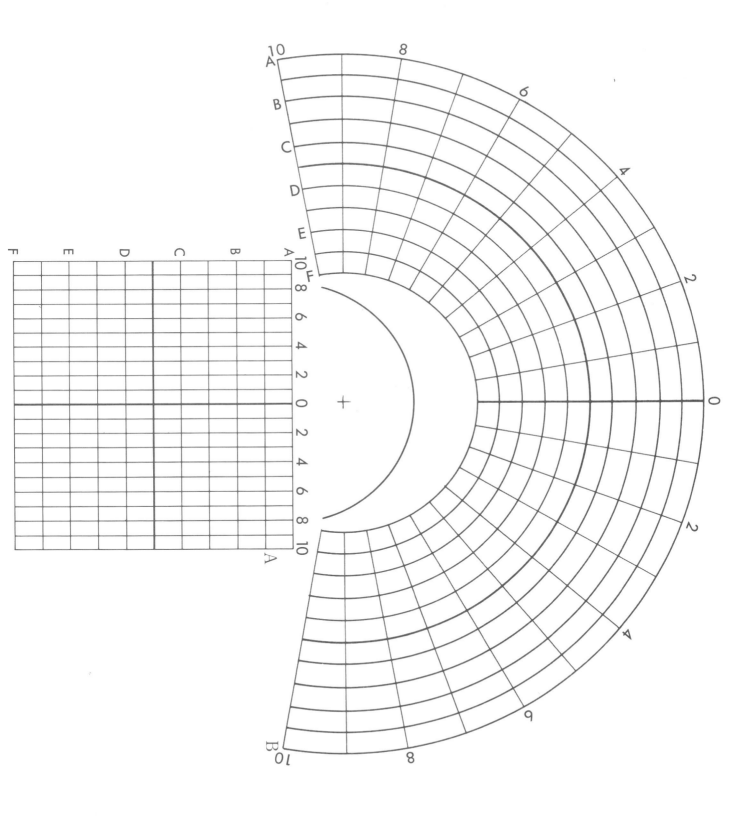

About Masaichiro Anno

Masaichiro Anno was born in Tokyo in 1954. He graduated from the National Science and Engineering Division of Waseda University in Tokyo and is now working in advertising.

Anno's Magical ABC was his idea. He drew the letters and his father, Mitsumasa Anno, wrote the text and drew the pictures. The picture on the left is a mixture of the body of Mitsumasa and the face of Masaichiro. Reflected in your mirror this man should look slim but if you think he looks a bit fat it must be because he is wearing such heavy clothes.

Clues to Anno's spells

A	Angel 天使	ant, anteater アリ、アリクイ	apple リンゴ
B	Balalaika バラライカ	bee, bear ハチ、クマ	blackberry クロイチゴ
C	Cassette カセットテープ	camel ラクダ	clover クローバー
D	Doll 人形	donkey ロバ	daisy デージー、ヒナギク
E	Elf, Egg 小びと、たまご	elephant ゾウ	elm ニレ
F	Faun フォーン牧神（ローマ神話の半人半羊の林野牧畜の神）ギリシャ神話ではPan	fox キツネ	forget-me-not ワスレナグサ
G	Glider グライダー	goat ヤギ	gentian リンドウ
H	House 家	horse ウマ	harebell (= bluebell) イトシャジン
I	Ice cream アイスクリーム	iguana イグアナ	ivy ツタ
J	Jack ジャック	jaguar ジャガー	jasmine ジャスミン
K	King キング	kangaroo カンガルー	knobble knapweed ヤグルマギクのなかま
L	Lamp ランプ	lion ライオン	lily ユリ
M	Mermaid 人魚	mouse ネズミ	millet キビ
N	Nut-cracker くるみ割り	newt イモリ	nettle イラクサ
O	Ocarina オカリナ	ox ウシ	oak カシの木
P	Pirate 海賊	pig ブタ	poppy ポピー、ケシ
Q	Queen クィーン	quail ウズラ	quince マルメロ
R	Racquet ラケット	rabbit ウサギ	rose バラ
S	Ship 帆船	squirrel リス	sun spurge トウダイグサ
T	Tricycle 三輪車	tiger トラ	thistle アザミ
U	Umbrella かさ	unicorn ユニコーン、一角獣	*urtica pilulifera* (= roman nettle) イラクサのなかま
V	Violin バイオリン	vulture ハゲタカ	violet スミレ
W	Windmill 風車	wolf オオカミ	walnut クルミの木
X	Xylophone 木琴	*xenus cinerius* (= terek sandpiper) ソリハシシギ	*xanthium strumarium* (= lesser burdock) オナモミ
Y	Yacht ヨット	yak ヤク	yew イチイ
Z	Zipper ジッパー	zebra シマウマ	zinnia ヒャクニチソウ

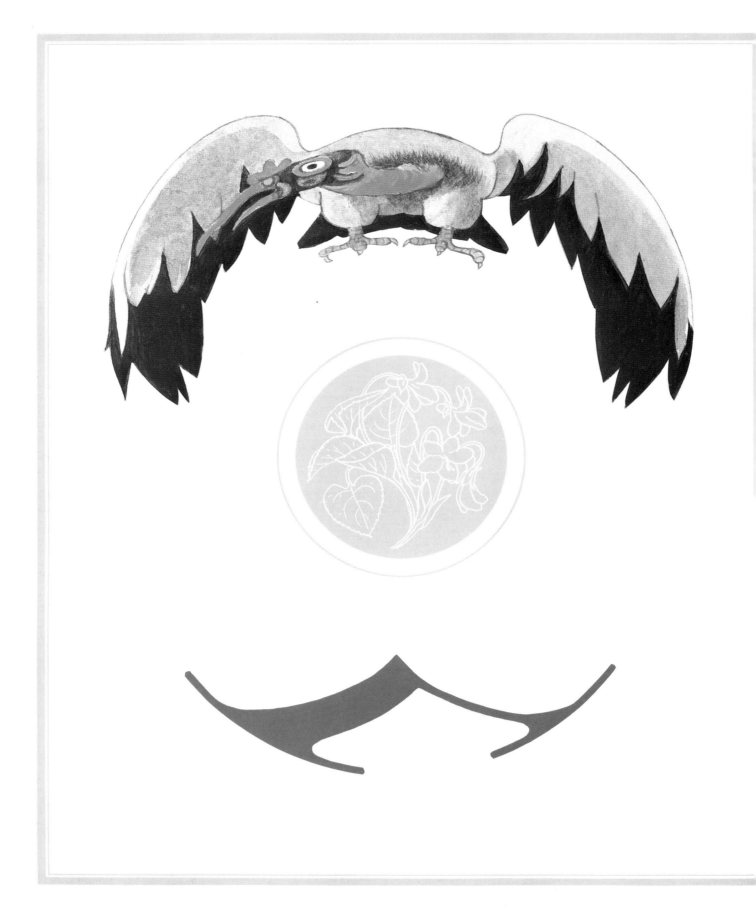

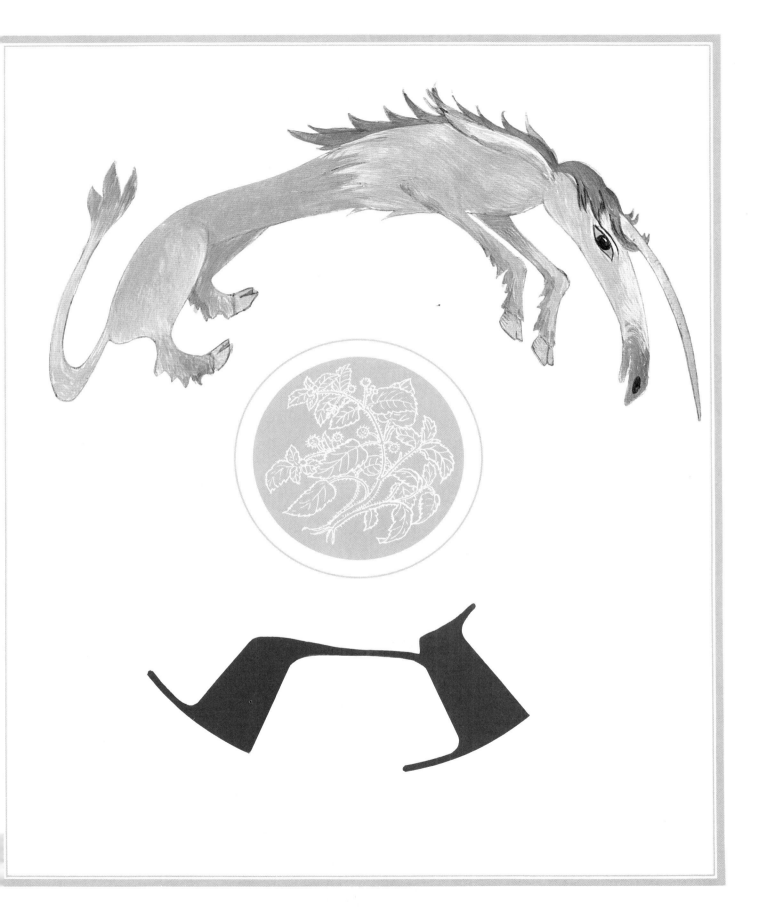

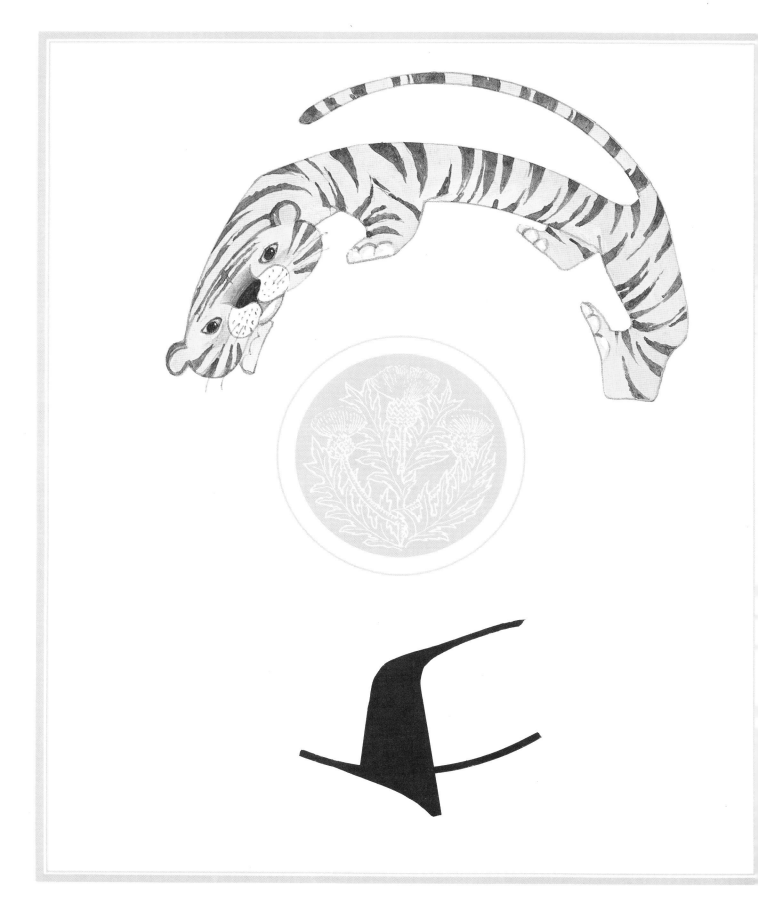

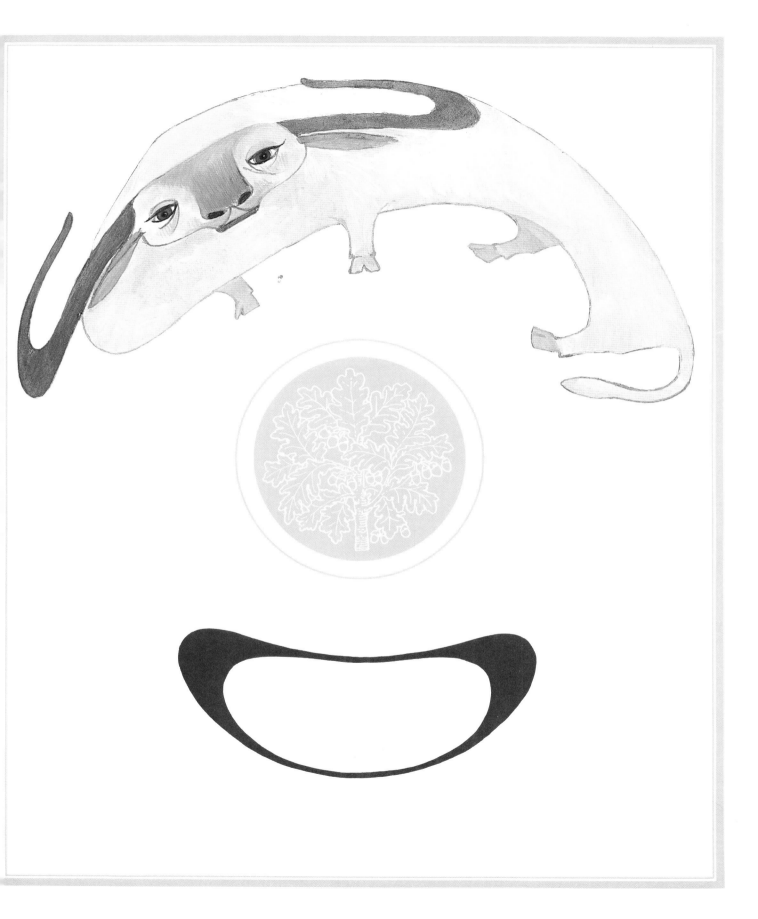

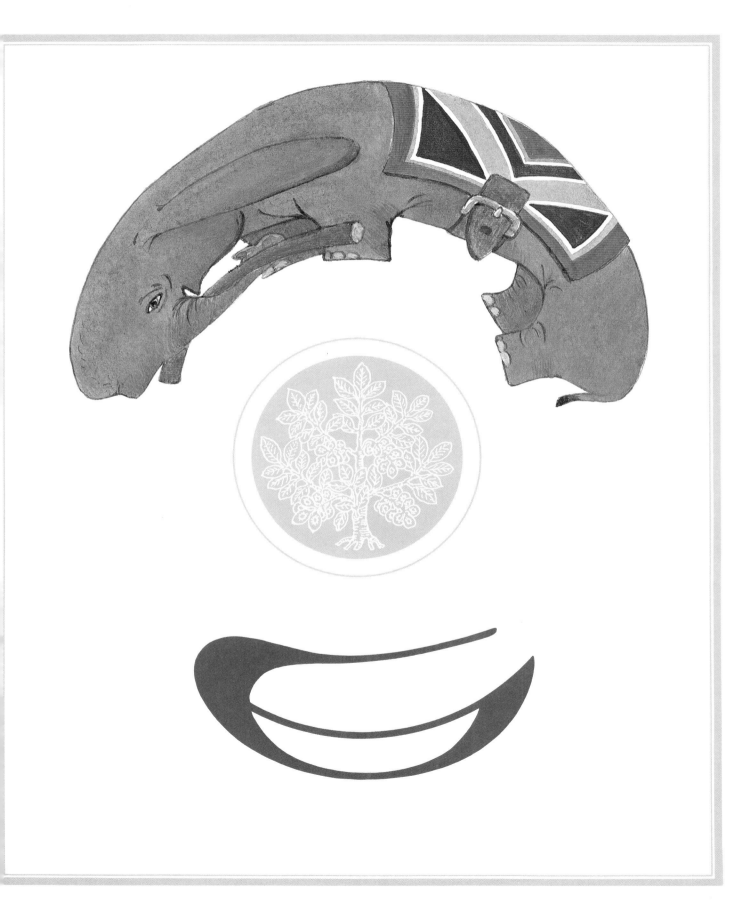

What is anamorphosis?

When you stand in front of a funny mirror in an amusement park the reflection of your face and body is distorted. In a concave mirror you look short and fat, in a cylindrical mirror you look tall and thin. The same is true, of course, of a reflected drawing or painting, and with a drawing or painting you can reverse the process. If you draw something warped and misshapen in a particular way and then look at it in a distorted mirror, its reflected image will look quite normal. This method of drawing is called anamorphosis and its purpose is solely to mystify and amuse.

The word anamorphosis seems first to have been used in the 17th century but the underlying principle of negative perspective was understood long before that by ancient Greek painters and sculptors who distorted the proportions of works designed to be exhibited in raised positions so that they would look normal when viewed from below. Anamorphosis was once very popular in Europe and two fine examples of anamorphosis in painting are the portrait of Edward VI in the National Portrait Gallery in London, attributed to Cornelis Anthonisz in 1546, and the distorted skull in Holbein's Ambassadors (1533) in the National Gallery in London. In Japan, too, during the Edo Period of 1600–1868 there was a type of anamorphic picture which was drawn to be reflected on the sheath of a sword. In the middle of this book you will find an explanation of how you can do your own anamorphic painting or drawing.

How to look at this book

Every new copy of *Anno's Magical ABC* has two sheets of mirror paper in a pocket inside the cover. Tape the paper around a drinking glass, an empty can, a bottle or a similar cylindrical object, and stand it in the middle of the page. Both the letter and the picture will spring into focus in the mirror. Keep the mirror paper clean by wiping it with a soft cloth.

If the original sheets of mirror paper have been used or lost, here are a number of alternative suggestions:
* Take the label off a can of soup (or baked beans or anything) and use the can as a reflector.
* Stand a new roll of aluminum foil in the middle of the page. It must be new because once the foil is unrolled it creases and spoils the reflection.
* Buy new sheets of mirror paper at an art supply shop, or stainless steel or aluminum sheets at a hardware shop.

Library of Congress Cataloging in Publication Data

Anno, Mitsumasa, 1926
Anno's magical abc.
SUMMARY: The distorted letters of the alphabet
become quite clear when viewed with the help of the
silver tube included with the book.
1. English language – Alphabet – Juvenile literature.
2. Anamorphic art – Juvenile literature. [1. Alphabet.
2. Toy and movable books] I. Anno, Masaichiro,
joint author. II. Title.
PE1155.A5 1981   421´.1   80–26024
ISBN 0–399–20788–0

Anno's Magical A B C
an anamorphic alphabet
Mitsumasa Anno & Masaichiro Anno

PHILOMEL BOOKS *NEW YORK*

DATE DUE